The Life Beside This One

Other books by Lawrence Raab

The Life
Beside
This One

L A W R E N C E   R A A B

Tᴜᴘᴇʟᴏ Pʀᴇss
North Adams, Massachusetts

Library of Congress Cataloging in Publication Control Number: 2017038947
ISBN: 978-1-946482-04-4

Cover and text designed and composed in Garamond and Trade Gothic by Howard Klein.
Cover art: "Le Rose Rosse" by Giorgio de Chirico (1888–1978). Tempera on canvas, 26 x
20 cm. Private collection. Copyright © 2017 Artists Rights Society (ARS), New York/SIAE,
Rome. Photo: Alessandro Vasari, courtesy of Mondadori Portfolio/Art Resource, NY.

First edition: November 2017.

Tupelo Press
P.O. Box 1767, North Adams, Massachusetts 01247
(413) 664-9611/editor@tupelopress.org/www.tupelopress.org

Tupelo Press is an award-winning independent literary press that publishes fine fiction,
nonfiction, and poetry in books that are a joy to hold as well as read. Tupelo Press is a
registered 501(c)(3) nonprofit organization, and we rely on public support to carry out
ourmission of publishing extraordinary work that may be outside the realm of the large
commercial publishers. Financial donations are welcome and are tax deductible.

ART WORKS.
arts.gov

Supported in part by an award from the National Endowment for the Arts

for Madeleine Deininger

Contents

*

*

*

*

*The people there aren't like us, but soon
it will be our turn.*

—a voice in a dream,
speaking about the past

The Life Beside This One

Women and the Sky

We were in Italy, my friend and I,
staying at *The Hotel of 1000 Strangers*,
when I got lost and wandered onto a golf course
bounded by a dark forest Dante would have
recognized. Back at the hotel someone

obviously famous was giving a lecture
on Swahili proverbs. "Who can understand
women or the sky?" he said, and paused
as if he wanted an answer. "Could that
involve two different people," I asked,

"one for the women and the other
for the sky?" "No," he replied, "and now
I would like to hear from someone else,
someone who has paid for this class."
Then I was lost again. I went into

a different hotel where some kind of party
was going on involving slabs of meat.
I asked the deskman, "Can you please
direct me to *The Hotel of 1000 Strangers*?"
"That hotel," he replied, "is much too far away."

"But I just came from there." "Well,"
he answered, "as the proverb says,
'A man who travels outside of time must enter
the dark woods where the dead still live.'"
"I don't want to do that," I told him.

"Alas, my friend, you have no choice."
Outside, a man who looked like Dante
from my old edition of the *Inferno*
asked me if I was ready. "Can you," I said,
"direct me to *The Hotel of 1000 Strangers*,

where even now my friend is waiting?"
"Are you in the middle of your life?"
Dante asked, and I said I was,
and he said, "Then it's the dark woods,"
and took hold of the edge of the cloak I seemed

to be wearing. "All right," I said, "but first,
tell me who can understand women or the sky."
He paused. "Is that women *or* the sky or women
and the sky?" "Well," I answered, "I think the *and*
is implied in the *or*, as in 'What one person

can understand both women and the sky?'"
"It's ambiguous," Dante replied, and I had to agree.
We started walking. "A man and the sky
are two," he told me. "A man, a woman,
and the sky are also two. That's part

of the answer. But now you must try
to understand what the dead understand."
"Why do I have to know that?" I asked.
We entered the woods. Darkness descended.
"Listen," he said. "It's time to stop fooling around."

Travelers

Meanwhile, she waited for her train
like the other travelers.
And though she thought
she perceived her situation clearly,
she couldn't help but wonder
how she had come to be at that station
at that hour, and with so little luggage.
Later there would be dreams.
And in one a valise might appear.
Then a forest, then a house
whose rooms were familiar but different
from any rooms in any house of her past.
Jean—that was her name—was now convinced
her train had been delayed.
She could inquire, make demands.
But she wished to conceal her feelings.
Someone might be watching,
or even, at that moment, about to arrive
with his excuses and satchel of letters
bound in packets by colorful ribbons.
Yet everyone around her
went about handing out the tickets,
arranging the flowers for sale,
as if nothing were amiss.
Jean could only imagine what they must be hiding.
Then her train appeared, barely
a minute late, or so she was told.
But as we know, such assurances
are frequently false, sometimes even

a kind of entrapment, leading you to believe
you can predict the future. And so
the conductor accepts the young woman's ticket.
Yes, Miss, he says, this is the train to the city,
the city whose name is stamped on your ticket,
the city you will enter alone and bereft,
though after that I can see no more.
Only your departure is visible,
because only your departure concerns me.

All Hallows

I seemed to be inside foreign worlds where there was some
kind of troubling camaraderie—as if a haunting joke was
known to everyone but me and yet faintly I knew it too.
—David Lynch, on a group of Halloween photographs

But I didn't know why they laughed
when they laughed. I had my suspicions—
that I was involved, even responsible.

There were boys in masks, girls in masks,
and often I couldn't tell the difference.
There were animals that were people,

and fires of bones. I wondered
if I was the only one without a mask,
and I was afraid to touch my face to find out.

They moved quickly through the shadows,
children as they seemed, while I
remained still, so they wouldn't suppose

I was one of the many who had
for just this night escaped from death
to trouble them, and be troubled.

Church bells rang, gates were hung in trees.
Apple peels, nut shells, and the sudden
flight of crows—all were part of the pattern

that was hidden in the joke that had
been kept from me, or forgotten by me,
or never understood by anyone in this world.

A Theory of Impossible Objects

First of all, do we need one? As you may recall,
the point of my last lecture, "A Theory of Invisible Objects,"
was that everything I was proposing was impossible,
however elegant the propositions might be:
the sound of the shirts being sewn, for example, ladders
lifted, water poured. None of that is relevant

when placed beside the absolute clarity of glass,
the air that holds nothing back, two hands
carefully cupping what isn't and cannot be there.
Many of you noticed, and some complained,
that all my lectures appear to be constructed
around absence, but what *isn't* rather than what *is*

is the philosopher's dream. Many of you
found this unconvincing, including, I am sorry to say,
the potential publisher of these lectures.
But so much fiddling around the edges
keeps me from my theory, from the splendid
central question of it. What exactly

do we need—more of the impossible or less?
I write things down and I think: yet another
useless document! And then I see the crows
suddenly fling themselves into the air
to scare the red-tailed hawk away from their nests.
This is remarkable, and if I have the wrong birds,

I'm sure I'll hear about it, although I'm reasonably
certain about the hawk. Now consider: A balloon!
A bicycle! A toaster! All impossible
according to my thinking, which I have
to assume those of you who are leaving
have already rejected. But too soon!

Now consider yourselves. Don't be afraid
to touch the absences around you.
Look at the shifting circles of light
on the grass beyond your window.
There they are! And then they aren't.
Something is always ending. You should know this.

Next Tuesday I will present my final lecture—
"A Theory of Insufficiently Impossible Objects"—
and I expect none of you to attend. Indeed,
most of you will have realized that philosophical theories
are best kept to oneself, and, ideally, I should speak
only to myself, which now happily seems to be the case.

An Education

"Isn't that just another way to feel compromised?"
Professor Heninger asked. Being freshmen
and mostly women as well, I was sure
we weren't being invited to disagree.
Then my mind wandered away and when
it came back, Professor Heninger was saying,
"Low expectations are the key to happiness,"
which made sense, however depressing
it was for me, a young person, to take to heart.
Not that I had any evidence that my expectations
should be high, though my parents were paying
a lot of money to believe otherwise.
"What do you *see*?" our professor hissed.
"What do you *feel*?" He had no reason
to be angry at me personally, so I decided
this must be part of his performance:
it was time to sound angry, or passionate.
I knew the girl in the second row
he kept addressing his thoughts to, and I figured
she was decoding them in an appropriate way.
"Time means *nothing*," he announced, and that
seemed important to him, although I
was of the opinion that time *was* important.
But for him it must have meant
getting older. And I felt sorry
that he didn't see that, or didn't see
that the girl in the second row, who was
in my dorm, knew exactly what was going on.
So much of this makes you think

that bad ideas *sound* like bad ideas,
which is, if I may say so, an education in itself.
And even if there are less expensive ways
of finding this out, it's worth keeping
in the back of your mind when anyone starts
lecturing you about time, or the truth,
or what it is you're supposed to be feeling.

Why the Past Is the Past

It's a weird feeling, Alice said, knowing
you can't go back, that the past is the past,
and I was thinking, Were you asleep
in English class all last week?
Isn't this a subject we covered?
Still, she was much too pretty to be spoken to
like that, and I knew what she meant
when she slid her hand into mine, or I slid mine
into hers, or it didn't matter, which was
the best interpretation. You know, she said,
what's done is done. And I had to agree.
But isn't that a good thing? I said.
Sometimes, Alice replied, throwing her hair back.
There were stars overhead. It was one
of those nights when many stars
were going on and off as the thin clouds
came and went. Alice, I said, remember
that green light at the end of the dock?
No, she replied, giving me a look
I couldn't read. I know, I know
I shouldn't have ruined the evening
by saying what I said then, though later
I wondered if anything could have happened
between us if she had actually
read the book. And I decided
that pretty as she was, my life would be close
to what it's become. No one
would envy me, or hate me enough

to shoot me, nor would I fall
into my swimming pool
and lie there as if I still couldn't help
loving the past.

Devotion

Suddenly the fire's out of control.
On the wall there's a Rembrandt,
and in the desk a snapshot
of your wife. Which one do you save?
The Rembrandt, of course.

But shouldn't you be facing
a serious moral dilemma?
Or at least a more difficult choice?

Then imagine that photo's the only one
left of your wife, who perished
in an earlier fire, along with all the negatives.
Say she was very beautiful.

Maybe you're thinking that's irrelevant.
But it's not. Beauty is never irrelevant.

So you rush back into the burning house,
at which point the entire second floor
collapses, and you're crushed,
grasping for the knob of the drawer.

A cruel irony? Not exactly.
More like an example of bad timing,
as well as a way of suggesting
this particular story has no moral
and no point, which is unfortunately

often the case with art today,
where lack of insight seems easily
confused with the world's apparent
absence of purpose—a common error,

I'm afraid, of the young,
who are so impatient, and thoughtless,
and beautiful, and impossible to save.

The High Note

A glass shatters when the woman sings
the high note in the song about love,
and how, once grasped,
love floats away like music, and is lost.
All of us are overcome

by this accomplishment,
and by the beauty of the woman
who has consented to sing,
and her white dress
that sparkles and distracts.

How suddenly the glass
flies apart, as if it were glad
to be released from its shape!
And yet how lovely it also was
only moments before,

cupping the wine that was poured
so carefully at the dinner
where the woman said, yes,
she could sing the note beyond
the note that keeps things whole.

But how fragile everything
already was, like the fleeting
habit of love, like the glass
I watched her raise,
then press to her lips.

Sad Robots

after a title by James Arthur

They were made to feel nothing
we take for granted. So if

we call them *sad*, that's only one
more example of what they, poor things,

can never comprehend. Warily
we watch as they pursue their daily

assignments—cleaning, making
the bed, pulling the sheets tight,

not noticing, as they mustn't,
anything like the grief of absence,

or the pleasures of solitude.
How we manage to get by

is beyond them, even when
we have to admit to each other

we feel the same. And yet
it was decided in their making

that what was ours
had to be protected: our passions

and our undoing, our not knowing
but forever wanting

someone who would.

Premonition

It seemed they were in a forest,

two children walking slowly
in some direction
they could not be sure of.

She wondered
if they might be imagining all of this,

as if they were traveling
through a story,
lost among the great trees

but about to be saved.

There was so much
to figure out. And this, she told
her brother, is why we need
to be cautious, yet unafraid.

Snow began to fall.

It seemed there was a path
that was meant to disappear,

and soon they would have to decide
whether or not to continue.

But that was when the dream ended—
before they had to choose.
And as the dreamer woke,
alone, in her own house,

she also felt lost, because
it was raining, and she understood—
the way we understand such things
when we haven't
yet wholly returned to the world—

that even if she found
her way back, the snow
would be too deep, the rain

too persistent, the keening
of the wind only the wind, rising and falling.

There would be no one she could save.

The Poem About the Henhouse

However hard you may try, there is never much to say about a henhouse.

—José Saramago

There it is. There are the hens
coming and going back into the house
to lay their eggs. Later they sleep.

There's more, but only if one knew
about hens and their houses, and even then
would there be much more to say?

So the wise writer turns elsewhere. Soon
he'll need an ordinary house and a yard
where children are happily playing

for all he can see, which causes him
to write that children's cruelty knows
no bounds, which is why the cruelty

of adults knows no bounds either.
Then he remembers his grandmother
telling him, "The world is so beautiful,

it makes me sad to think I have to die."
Even the henhouse is beautiful,
and its rickety fence, the fields also

and dry gullies, and the hills bearing up
under the sun, and the amazement
of the sky above them all.

A Difficult Assignment

for and after Stephen Dunn

You'll need an adjective for bedroom,
another that makes the forest you keep returning to

seem run-down, a kind of bad neighborhood.
Then an adjective before "path," which changes

the meaning of it, as if you weren't going to end up
where you planned. Or the opposite—

you can't help where you're going.
And where would that be? It's up to you,

but in all of this you should be alone
although at some point a woman must appear,

throwing everything into question.
That's when the false note rings true.

Maybe she has something to say about Cedar Rapids
or Muddy Waters. She's imaginary,

she can say anything you want. Yes,
how much she desires you is one kind of beginning,

but another might involve looking carefully
at those flowers at the edge of the forest, asking her

their names, then suggesting you don't care
where the path leads if that's where she wants to go.

Climbing the Mountain

The weather looks like a problem
but your friends decide to climb
the mountain anyway. Come with us,
they say, but you say you have work to do,
plus you don't want to get caught in a storm.

You don't tell them you have no interest
in climbing any kind of mountain.
Then the dark clouds are suddenly swept away.
They have a great time, see all five states
from the summit, return giddy and flushed.

Or else it rains, nothing but drizzle at the top,
and they still have a great time, which you
know they'll be talking about forever:
Remember when we climbed the mountain,
and Lily said, and then Nick said…

Or maybe everything goes wrong:
fog, bugs, blisters. No one's worn the right
kind of shoes. Lily wants to turn back,
Nick wants to go on. This is the version,
you can't help remarking, that's closest to life—

messy, unfocused, completely lacking
a persuasive dramatic center.
No! you hear Nick crying out. Give me a break!
And Lily adds: It wasn't like that at all.
It was fine. You should have come with us.

Mirror Lake

Remember when we first met in that hotel
in the woods by the lake that was so clear
Mirror Lake might have been its name?
Or something with a word like "stillness"
inside it. Some kind of hush. But I digress.
I want to say that in your most recent letter
you seem like such a different person—
no one, that is, who would hold a lot
of insane points of view, which is
what struck me back then as we rocked
on the porch watching the water
settle down, and you explained how the world
was about to end, but not for all of us.
And how you could be sure of the essence
of my soul by the light around my body—
whether it was purple or green.
And therefore if I was destined to survive
the times ahead. I listened
for as long as I could, and when
I left I believe I was not unkind,
even if I thought: Well, kindness alone
can't change the way I feel.
I'm writing now to say I believe
your ideas are still as crazy as they come,
but I miss them, as I miss those evenings
of watching the darkening lake and hearing—
whenever you stopped talking—
a couple of loons calling across the wide
and lonely stillness of the water, not to us,
as you once said, but to each other.

Animals That Didn't Make It into the Ark

"The storm's picking up," I told my wife.
"Maybe it will rain all night."
"Maybe," she replied, "it will rain
for forty days and forty nights,
until the world is clean." I figured
she was joking, but it reminded me
how sorry I'd always felt for the animals
that didn't make it into the ark. Why
should they suffer for the sins of men?
I could see the horses struggling to stay afloat,
and the owls and meadowlarks giving up
and slipping into the waves. I wondered
what Mrs. Everwine would have said
had I brought this up in Sunday School.
I believe she would have folded her hands
and told me gently that if I insisted
on upsetting the younger children
I should go out into the hall by myself.
But what about the rabbits? I could hear
the children asking. What about
the chipmunks and the squirrels?
Some of them were starting to cry.
Then the storm was over—nothing but wisps
of fog decorating the mountains,
not even the briefest shimmer
of a rainbow. "Don't forget,"
my wife replied, having understood
my thoughts, "you're an atheist.
You should be having a lot more fun."

A Few Words About the Moon

As soon as we arrived at the ruins
I had my doubts,
but what can you do
when you've followed the woman you love
so far into the jungle you know
she's convinced that once the moon
has risen the spirits will appear—some
of great delicacy, she said, others feverish
and wild. Which wasn't always
the way she talked, as if she'd really
been listening to the dead, or hadn't
noticed the natives approaching
with their blowguns and spears.
When I suggested we might consider
leaving, she claimed
I was timid and dull and had been
since the day we met.
I'd never known she felt that way.
And it disheartened me
more than I wanted her to see.
Meanwhile, the moon was turning the ruins
into white cascades of stone.
There were furtive rustlings
in the brush, and I could make out
members of our group slipping into the shadows.
"Darling," I said, "it's time to go."
"But we just got here," she replied,
as if we were at a party
where everyone was talking about jungles
and temples where you could stand

at a certain hour with your wife and feel
the astonishment of having just met,
and of being unable to imagine
anything to say except, perhaps,
a few words about the beauty of the moon.

The Logical Level

"Perhaps you mean—lowest possible 'logical' level?"
asked Tentarelli. "No," I replied, restraining myself
admirably, "that's not what I mean at all." I'd heard
the quotation marks around "logical," and I knew
everyone in the room knew what that meant.

But Tentarelli was the mayor and I couldn't attack him,
by which I mean, say what I was really thinking—
that he was a fucking idiot who understood
nothing about logic but was keenly aware I hadn't
voted for him. And about Tentarelli's claim

in the next election that he'd never taken
cash under the table—we all knew he had.
So I said it, so he sued, so I hit him,
which made me sorry because there were
too many witnesses. That last part happened

long after the meeting, but I often get time
mixed up. Like exactly when I moved here,
and who said I'd better find some quiet town
like your town, and stay there. Sure, I'd still
like to make Tentarelli aware of his mistakes,

and in some way that would harm him
a little more than he harmed me.
But I've made no plans. My philosophy
is to lie low, just wait and see.
On the other hand, don't believe

anyone who says I want to hurt *you*.
You've given me reason, yes,
but there are reasons for everything in life,
and a man's got to let most of them go.
Unless he can't. Unless he has to act.

Another Case of Spontaneous Combustion

I rushed into the house and found Hammond ablaze on the couch.
Was this truly an example
of "spontaneous combustion"? Such occurrences,
I'd read, happened often
beside the sea, but rarely inside on a couch. So Hammond,
perhaps, had merely fallen asleep
while smoking. Or else designed his spectacular end
as a protest, though against what
I could not imagine. Or else he'd decided he'd had
enough of life, and I
could sympathize with that. But now I saw
Hammond was beyond
hope, beyond the need to summon me
to listen to his last words,
if he'd even considered what words those might be.
What could I do
but try to save the house? Then it began to rain,
the soft, gauzy rain
of spring that would not help. When the firemen arrived
they said the house
was fully engaged. When Hammond's girlfriend
arrived she said it didn't matter,
they'd broken up last week following a long argument,
the details of which
she refused to reveal. Walking home
I tried to remember
if I'd ever been in the position
of rescuing anyone.
No, I decided, there was only Hammond,

and he was too mysterious
to have offered me the chance
to save his life,
or to wonder if I could do it,
or even if I should.

Replicas

We were tooling along in Fred's old jalopy,
thrown off our game
because the directions to the lunatic asylum were confusing.
I decided not to mention how appropriate
getting lost might be, maybe later

having to battle the elements to stay alive.
I'd been reading the old myths
and liked to imagine sailing through the clashing rocks
with only an oar for a weapon,
which wasn't the most useful idea since we were heading

south of Tampa, trying to find our old friend
Adam, who might be waiting for a visit.
On the other hand, I thought, and then recalled
Adam having said far too often: *On the other hand—
a knife is up close and personal.*

People didn't like to hear that kind of thing,
but we were sure he meant no harm,
even if in fact he did. We figured by now
he'd have forgotten the dangerous inclinations
of his youth, those days when he insisted

we'd all been misled by the voices
in our heads, then turned into replicas
of the people we thought we were. "Of course,"
Adam explained, "certain men choose
to be tempted by sirens. Others just let it happen."

I told Fred that last part made sense, or sounded
like it should. "Damn," Fred replied,
having taken another wrong turn.
"Not every kind of craziness makes sense.
Believe me, you've got to draw the line somewhere."

At first Adam was upset about being sent away,
but since then we'd heard
he'd grown accustomed to the quiet gardens
they let him putter about in. We imagined
him kneeling down in the soil

like his namesake and weeding
something small and green,
wondering why he'd ever believed
what he had, or else why no one
had ever understood what he believed.

Or perhaps both thoughts vanished
while he concentrated on his task, half-listening
to the murmuring of the more distracted guests
as they explained to each other how easily
they had been deceived by their lives.

Emptiness of the Air

He was killed by a book. It fell
heavily from his highest shelf
as he fumbled for another beside it,
and knocked him to the floor, senseless,
after which he stood beside himself,
looking down, a ghost already.

What was the name of that book?
Perhaps the subject was ghosts,
if death had chosen to be ironic.
But when he tried to find out
his hand passed through
whatever he touched as if through air.

Soon his body would be discovered
and suddenly he needed to be
far away from anyone's shock
or grief. So he drifted off—
he could drift—as ghosts in a fiction
drift through the walls of their houses.

Then he was outside watching his wife
pruning the lilacs.
And the world was still,
but all the things that had been his
he could not bear to see,
since he could no longer touch them.

For days he wondered about the name
of the book that had struck him down,
and if anyone there had remarked
on the absurdity of that moment.
A *book*, after all! But soon
he began to consider

the life of a ghost. What should I want?
Must I return to haunt my house
and worry my family? Will I ever
vanish entirely? No one explained,
and then it seemed like years
since his death, and perhaps it was.

He grew thin, and sad,
until he could not recall how sadness
should feel. No one at all, he realized,
is what ghosts must become
when finally they are forgotten.
So it didn't matter, he thought,

about the unknowable
subject of that book, or even how much
others may once have cared for him.
All of it was slipping
away into time
as if into the emptiness of the air.

Continuous Life

after Mark Strand

What are early mornings for
if not to notice that the dust on the roads
has not yet started to rise, or the trees
to press against each other as the wind advances,
or someone to walk toward you
carrying a piece of paper upon which
the history of the future has been written,
the one in which we are all saved from ourselves,
and then step outside, a few at a time, to marvel
at the improbable distance this light has traveled
to show us what he, without insistence,
allowed us to see.

Whatever You Want to Believe

Next to an unknown, place a known.
—Camille Corot

Inside the space she once ran through
place the dog, and above her
the red ball that will no longer descend.

In the dark, place a switch.
In the night, try the moon,
then a cloud to disguise it.

Why not trust what is hidden?
—a single flake of snow
inside a drift of snow, water

under the bridge, as if everything
could be compared to time, or a river,
or just itself. Why not assume

that what makes you happy
is necessary, that making things
is only as futile as making nothing.

So above the ball above the dog,
place whatever kind of sky
you don't want to worry about.

And beyond it
whatever you want to believe.
It doesn't have to be true.

Sunrise with Sea Monsters

after J. M. W. Turner

There they are, surprisingly pink,
although the rising sun may contribute
to that effect. We who live here
know them only as you see them now,
a shifting of colors as they lift
their backs above the ocean.
Look at their eyes, so large
and impassive, as if we should understand
something we don't. So we wonder,
calling them monsters because
no one's given them a better name.
And because they frighten us, as monsters should.
You saw them quite clearly, didn't you?
Later, back home, maybe
you'll decide it was all a trick of the light,
and I was the one who persuaded you
they were real. But I just bring people
out here to the cliffs where they see
what they see and believe whatever fits
the stories they want to tell.
Some say we should kill them.
Others would build them a shrine.
What I know is—they appear,
let us look, and are gone. Or else
it's all just the light, the rising sun like an eye
—the eye of God, I once heard a man say—
staring right through us, burning away
everything we thought we knew.

The Madman's Laughter

What does he want this time?
What he always wants—
the world to bend to his wishes.
And how, exactly?
For that you must ask him,

but being mad
he will always tell you
a different version of the truth.
Sometimes it's a song
no one can resist,

and sometimes it's a woman
he loves or hates so much
he can't help but lie to himself.
Listen to him,
carrying on in his room

as if he owned the world
and truly believed
he could make the fiercest beast
come to him
and the lion lie down with the lamb.

The Prophet's Certainty

I'd like to believe
I could be wrong,
that what I have to tell you
is only my opinion,
as inconsequential
as all the other opinions
that every day you can't avoid.
I understand you've heard
about the end of the world too often
from the false and crazy
men in the street, the ones
who just want a dollar for food.
They don't know how
to embrace their hunger
as I do, or be alone
as I must be alone.
But even if I were to stand on a pillar
in the desert for years and change
no one's mind,
I wouldn't be mistaken
about the future,
and the terror of it, and the fierce
and awful beauty
I shouldn't be sorry
I can't make you see.

What Death Said

After a while, one late afternoon
as I was walking beside the sea,
I heard Death say, "I'll tell you a secret.
Don't be surprised, but any theory
you invent to account for me

will be true. Not entirely true,"
he added, "but true enough."
So I thought I would ask:
Does that mean I can prove
your powers are useless, your promises

a fraud, your presence a mere illusion?
"All of that and more," said Death,
who had been listening to my thoughts.
"But in the end whatever
you devise you will disown."

We walked a little farther, looking around
at nature. But what was lovely was lovely
only until it wasn't. Which was no help.
"No help at all," said Death, "is it?"
So then I thought of dying at peace in my bed.

"Alas," said Death. And the sea
wore against the shore. And the birds
of that region were finishing their songs.
I could think of nothing else to think.
"You see the problem," Death said.

"But since you've read so much
about me, remember—I have no reason
to deceive you. Which is why
I'm pleased you walked this far with me
as if it were your choice."

Everything That Isn't Happening Here

is happening elsewhere. All kinds of cruelty,
for example, all kinds of astonishment.
Like the pear tree in my friend's front yard—
how delicately the leaves are turning,
how long the tree waits to reveal its colors.
And then there are the dreams
we can't remember most of—a black satchel
full of tools, rain in a window, the flare
of a match. With tomorrow comes
winter's first ice, bending the branches
of the vulnerable trees, wrenching them
from their sockets. Earlier than last year,
we say, but we may have forgotten.
When I stopped reading the papers
and watching the news, I didn't
miss it, which doesn't mean
I don't feel bad casting my vote
for ignorance. Elsewhere most people
can't afford a lawn and a pear tree.
And there are plagues
and ever-more-terrible storms
I don't want to see the pictures of.
And the voices of those who will not
make it home. Elsewhere
water bursts into flame because
it's happened before and will again.
And the sky refuses to be still,
as if it wished to be released from the duties
it once performed—watching over us

like the blue curves of the dome of heaven.
Life is short, Andrei Platonov wrote.
There is not enough time to forget everything.

Let Me Tell You What to Feel

I can tell you're not sure
if I'm really your friend, or someone
from the other side. What would
convince you to trust me?
I know everything
that's gotten to you—what they've done
to the ocean, and the fish in the ocean,
and the people on the shore.
I understand, and I feel
the same, and I can't do anything
about it either. But right now
the sky's blue enough, the trees
are holding their own, and the dogs
are told to *hush* when they bark too often.
Imagine that *hush*, like the sound
of snow falling all around a man
who's so tired he says to the angels,
Come on down. Even if he doesn't
believe in them, he's dying in the snow
that swirls around him and looks enough
like angels to make him think
he might be wrong. If you were he,
what would you want me to tell you?
Hush, I'd say. *Look at the angels
bending down to lift you up,
you who did not want to believe
they were on your side.*

Five Parables

1.   LILIES OF THE FIELD

You knew she was a saint because the birds trusted her.

And the flowers in the fields
leaned in her direction as if wishing to be blessed,
although they might have been saying,

We ask for nothing but what we have,
which is why we are not anxious for our lives.

You wanted to be different,
but look at yourself—you are the same as your father.

And absence?
Doesn't it drive everything into your dreams?

Doesn't it only pretend to release you?

And when Death explains
what you must become, you reply:
But you believe in only one kind of destiny.
And Death replies: I believe in everything.

And the ghost of your father says:
Take your longing away—
it won't help either of us now.

Which is why men cling to the idea of change.

Consider the lilies of the field—
how God so loves them that even
the greatest king could never be arrayed
like one of these.

Look how the quiet morning
allows them to live,
how the woman pauses among them,
how chance troubles them as little as fate,

since unlike yourself
they do not dream
nor are they anxious for their lives.

2. A MAN AT MIDNIGHT

Imagine a man at midnight knocking
on your door, asking for bread.

If you knew
he was Christ and yet you rejected him,
how could you not help
but feel ashamed, then later wonder
why, of all those asleep, you had been chosen.

But you knew nothing.

You might have been dreaming
of your father
standing outside your house.

Perhaps he was about to speak—
to forgive you, or to ask
for your forgiveness.

My door is shut, you call out.
It is midnight. My children are asleep.
I have nothing to give you.

And today, in the casual light
of morning, you wonder:
But why should I be blamed
if I didn't understand, and was afraid

waiting in the darkness
for the knocking to cease?

3.   THE FIG TREE

The fig tree is in bloom, therefore summer
is almost upon us.

Look at the wind tear at the branches

as if the tree
were not meant to survive,
or had to prove it could

to enter the weather of August,
to become
part of everything that is briefly calm.

This generation will not pass away
until all things are accomplished,
Christ said. But in this he was mistaken.

Why not believe in postponement?

Of course you want to live.
You want to live forever.

That's how the tree becomes part of the story.
The gardener shows his patience,
although his patience has limits.

But now it is still spring,
so the question cannot be answered.

If the figs ripen the tree will be saved.
If not, it will be cut down.

What, after all, could it represent
except yourself?

4.   Legion of Demons

The legion of demons and the suicidal swine
came much later.
What I recall is simple—just a few words
and our friend was himself again.

For months madness
had overwhelmed him with certainty.
We weren't surprised.

What is madness, after all,
but certainty about everything?
And he was already
inclined in that direction.

Then he explained
that he could see by our faces
who each of us was pretending to be,
and more often than not he was right.

After which
no one wanted to hear
his prophecies and premonitions—

neither his wife nor his children,
who wept for the changes he'd embraced,
nor his neighbors, who were fearful,
nor the strangers on the road
he stopped to exhort, nor the soldiers
who mocked him.

He forgave them all, since that was part of his madness.

And in this way
life continued, until one of the many
prophets of those days, passing through

with his followers,
paused, and knelt down, and said
something we couldn't hear, and our friend

blinked his eyes in astonishment,
and was as he had been.

Later, when word got around
about the multitude of demons
he'd been possessed by,
and the two hundred swine rushing off
into the sea to escape from that evil,

there was no doubt
how much drama this prophet,
or one of his disciples,
had added to our lives.

And why not?
A savior needs his miracles to be impressive.

We understood.

After all, our friend had been restored
and was again
like the rest of us,
a man who knew what we all knew—
the stuff of day by day,
world without end, enough to get by.

5.   House of Sand

He'd asked me to go with him to the sea.

He wasn't about to walk upon the water.
He just wanted me to look, and tell him what I saw.

So I said I saw the colorful sails
of those boats near the horizon,
and the small waves on the shore,
and two children building
a house from the sand.

Surely they realize
the tide will take away whatever they make.
And yet tomorrow, I said,
the children may return.

The scent of oranges drifted down to us
from the hills. He told me
that what I needed to know I knew.

And I did not reply
because I was certain
the secret of that moment had escaped me.
And I thought if I said what I felt
—that he was wrong—
he would leave me.

Perhaps that was my error.

But shouldn't he have recognized how much
my desire to believe
crippled me—
so that I saw only what anyone would see?

Death's Many Special Agents

Try to pick us out in a crowd, any of us,
all of us—strangers, neighbors,
your best friend. You can never

get it right, seeing only
who we've chosen to be.
Now picture everything you've heard

about the basements where we operate—
how no one returns
to his family, or is allowed

to stay the same. It's all true.
Does it give us pleasure? Listen—
what happens has to happen.

Didn't our children once play together?
Didn't we watch them in the park
as the leaves of the oaks

were beginning to fall? You may not
have noticed, but I remember those days.
How glad you were just to be there.

The End of Certainty

Whereas today's discourse of experience turns on
the phrase, "in my experience ...," nineteenth-century
American experience turns on phrases such as,
"A man, looking upon a scene, will feel ..."
—Theo Davis

At first, looking upon the river, he feels
satisfied, because it is his river,
his fields as well, unfurling on either side.
Then he hesitates, wondering
if those distant hills, which belong

to someone else, might be
a symbol of the future—how fate
some day could change his life completely.
From where he stands he can barely see
the curl of smoke from his house,

can only imagine his family inside.
How much he loves them,
and yet how hard it is, sometimes,
to love them. And what if he were
called upon to travel a great distance?

One should feel only what is right,
the man thinks, standing on that hill
in Massachusetts, in the middle
of the nineteenth century. One should
not guess about such things, or have to wonder.

Problems of Levitation

I tried hard all morning and around noon
thought I'd risen just a little, but I had no proof.
And to make things worse, a few days ago
my wife said she'd seen through my idea

that this was some new kind of yoga.
"I know what you're up to," she told me.
"Holy men," I remarked, as she left,
"have often been known to levitate."

I'd seen the pictures. And they looked
so calm—those saints and yogis—
as if in a very advanced state of knowledge,
having discovered the peace they'd searched

for all their lives. The point is my marriage
was coming apart because of my desire
to float in space, which, as desires go,
is certainly not dangerous, although yesterday,

following yet another failed attempt to rise
to the ceiling, I found her crying in the bathroom,
and I didn't know what to say, since levitation
seemed so silly compared to her tears,

while at the same time her tears seemed
inconsequential compared to levitation.
"Soon," I said, "I'm sure you'll see
for yourself." After that she took the dog

and moved out. Which is why I feel
so sorry I have no way to show her
that this morning I slowly rose above
the pale blue couch she chose for us shortly

after we married, when we were both happy,
almost as happy, I thought, as I am right now,
adrift in the air above our couch, which looks
so different from the way I saw it then.

It Appeared There Was a Story

All morning I wanted to do nothing
but lie on the bed and wait
for the pain in my chest to subside,
the pain I kept telling myself wasn't serious,
more like a small metallic bird, trapped inside,
fluttering its wings now and then.
It didn't want to hurt me, it wanted to get out.
But I just felt like closing my eyes,
being very quiet, and in this half-life
of a dream it appeared there was a story
I was supposed to enter to find
someone who needed my help.
All this took place in the past, and a voice
almost like my own told me:
The people there aren't like us, but soon
it will be our turn. The wings of the bird
brushed my skin. It was time to ask
who was in danger and what I should do,
but when I turned to face them they were gone.
A vast prairie lay before me.
In the distance men were riding
furiously through great plumes of dust,
and as they drew closer the light struck
the silver barrels of their guns, so I could tell
something important was about to happen.
But the bird in my chest reminded me
to be still. *This story isn't about you.*
Just lie here a while longer
and let me find my way back into the air.

In the Natural World

Animals dream, but of what we do not know.
They wake quickly, even when accustomed
to safety. Maybe some think back, maybe

others are anxious. But what about regret?
Does it play a part in their kingdom?
Or is it only our burden? In one night

moles can dig tunnels 200 feet long,
while all that time we're awake
brooding about the future,

which makes sense, or the past,
which is hopeless, or about the moment
itself as we lie there, letting a few

more minutes slip away into an hour,
then another, as if there were nothing
to being awake but losing, which is not

a thought animals entertain,
however inconsolable they might appear,
bent over their dead and their dying.

Invisible

When an invisible man walks into a room
everything shines through him.
If he's a little blurry around the edges,
it's a sign these experiments
never work completely, although visions
of great power will always warp a man's mind
and harden his heart. When a ghost appears

often a secret has been keeping it
bound to the earth. Usually a house
is part of the reason—spirits of children
lost in the hallways, rooms that refuse
to give up the cries of those
who once lived, and still weep.
They all need to rest, to shut their eyes.

An invisible man laughs at the world,
and the world is afraid. But he's human,
he can be hurt. Lightning splits open
the poisonous house, releasing
its prisoners. Sleep returns. Death
closes his book, and once again the invisible
is everything that just isn't there.

Being a Monster

Being a monster, he merely wished
to assuage his loneliness.
    —Kōbō Abe

You talk about disappointment,
the insinuating perfume
of the last woman to leave you.
You say listening to yourself think
is another way of losing hold,
that you live surrounded
by the logic of terrible mistakes.
But it isn't easy
to remain convinced that every part
of the world can be used against you,
that loneliness, real loneliness,
won't ever desert you, but will change
into a kind of comfort. Trust me.
This is what I know, living where
I've always lived, inside a body
you'd tremble to imagine.
Which is why you want to imagine me
and tremble. To feel certain
you and I share almost nothing.

The Howling

Every year there's always an incident or two,
sometimes more. I don't want to go into the details—
you want the details, ask my friend Shirley. You want
drama, ask my husband Mike. And if you want
just about nothing, keep talking to me.

Okay, there's the rain and the fog, and the howling
in the woods, which at first we didn't
pay much attention to since it never seemed
closer than the day before. And no worse
than our stupid neighbor's dog

at the end of his chain—now don't get me started
on dogs, none of whom get enough respect
around here. But that's not what was howling.
Or broke all those small trees in half. Or took away,
if you have to know, at least one of us. So—

you ask me if there's stuff out there
I don't understand and I say, Shit yes,
and a whole lot of it, which is why we stay
on the main roads now, don't go far into the woods,
or wander alone beside the sea. Of course

that girl could have slipped and fallen
and the riptide took her away, but that's not what
some folks think took her away. That's why
they're afraid, and need to keep their secrets,
which I should have kept to myself today,

because the bottom line is that the world
isn't happy to have us in it. And if you want
to quote me on that one, go ahead.
But leave the rest of it alone. No one wants
to be reminded of what they can't have back.

A Difficult House to Sell

Well, these look like tiny bedrooms to me,
the husband said, and how could I argue, wedged up
as we were against the walls. And the ceilings,
his wife added, aren't they a little low? Yes,
a little, I had to admit, all of us stooped over
and peering through the single dusty window
at the hedges that blocked our view of the water.
And what *about* the view? the husband asked
rather testily. It's out there, I told him.
Just because you can't see something clearly
doesn't mean you need to. Anyway,
a few adjustments to the plantings will do it,
let you feel right next to nature if that's
what you want. It's not what I would want,
but don't be concerned about me.
As for the bedrooms—*cozy* is certainly
the word, and *intimate*, like every one
of the other rooms, which is the reason
the shrubbery has been allowed—
no, *trained*, I would say—to admit so little sun.
And that's why you should ask yourselves,
Do I want to be overwhelmed by the darkness
or the light? Well, said the husband,
I'm not sure. Don't decide, I told them,
until you are. Look, I explained,
shouldn't a house keep life
at a reasonable distance, allowing you to survey
things from a position of safety?

Then, when you're ready, let the world come to you. Let it knock on your door like a stranger, pleading to be let in.

I Wanted to Think He Was Happy

I'd thought he was already dead
when I read in the papers that he'd died.
Then I thought I should feel sorry
about my mistake, the way in my mind
I'd denied him many years of pleasure,

or just of growing older and watching
the world change. Had he believed
he'd be, right now, in a better place?

Had he worried about the details?
Like which of his several wives
might again be his wife, or if marriage
was even an issue after death.

Then it was time for lunch
with my friend Ralph, who even before
we sat down asked me if I'd seen
that so-and-so had died. "I thought
he was already dead," I said.

"Maybe," said Ralph, "he was
as good as dead." But now
I wanted to think he was happy
right up until the end,

when he drifted off without pain or remorse.
I hadn't known him, and didn't understand
my desire to wish him well,

but the feeling swept over me
that I was writing a story
and could do whatever I wanted
with everyone in it. I felt

like a prophet, who would be allowed
to see the promised land
but only from afar, since the creator

must remain behind,
looking back over his work:
how he could have done it better,
what it was now too late to change.

The Afternoon Lesson

"Always," Mr. Crumley said, "always
be prepared to go to a dark place."
We were just kids, but finally Joan
asked why. "I'm disappointed, Joan,"
Mr. Crumley replied, "that you have to ask,
but I understand. For now, however,
just trust me on this one." After that

no one spoke up. "We'll go into it all
in more detail later," Mr. Crumley said.
"But first it's time to learn about owls."
This didn't seem like a bad idea, given the options.
"Owls," Mr. Crumley said, "are passionate
and deceptive. They also mate for life.
In many ways they are like us, but better,

since they leave us alone, whereas we—
but you know how we treat each other.
Which is one reason to know when to hide,
which we'll go into later. In the meantime,
never get between a mother bear and her cubs.
Never do that. But enough about the natural world."
This seemed like a short lesson,

shorter than most. I was going to ask
if we'd be tested on the material, but I didn't.
I think we were all feeling a little uneasy
that afternoon. "Now it's time,"
Mr. Crumley said, "for each of you to draw a map.

Making one up is the point of this task.
For example, the map I'd personally want

would refuse to confirm my suspicions
about where I was, or might be going, or what
I could expect to happen when I got there.
See what you can do. Naturally, I don't
expect perfection, but a little imagination
goes a long way in my book."
He handed out paper and colored pencils.

"And now," he said, "I'm feeling a little under
the weather, so I'll just sit behind my desk
for a while, and think about my life."
I'm sure we were all sorry that he was so tired,
because in fact we liked Mr. Crumley,
strange as he could be, and I know
that none of us, with the possible exception

of Roger, wanted to believe
we were responsible for his weariness,
which I could see was a sadness as well,
both for himself and for us, for our futures,
how some day we might need
to hide in a dark place, and be afraid,
though of what we had not yet been told.

Until Evening

Repeating themselves, the seasons
become, each year, more symbolic.

In the winter there are huge piles of snow.
In the summer: water lilies.

Summer ends and returns.
We ourselves return, and even if

this hillside conceals another,
in the distance a mountain appears

with its sharp peaks and icy ridges,
now impassible. You're tired,

aren't you? You'd like to build a fire
and let the snow accumulate, forget

about the shovels by the door.
Or, if it were summer, you might

sit quietly on the bank by the pond
and watch the water lilies—

how they don't change, although
if you stayed long enough, if you waited

until evening, and then the end of evening,
you would see them shiver and close.

Swimming in the Air

A bat appears, zigzagging across
the twilight, indifferent
to its freedom, and I'm reminded
of the dream where I float

out of my bed and up to the ceiling.
When I move my arms, the air
could be water, although I never try
to slip through a window into the dark.

I'm not frightened. Going outside
simply doesn't occur to me.
Do I understand what this means?
No, the dream is sufficient—

the pleasure of swimming in the air
before I descend into myself—
which I know is where I should be,
while from the other side of the door

my father is asking,
*Haven't you had enough fun
for one night?* But it's not
a question, and I never answer.

What You Lose in Sleep You Gain in Mortal Danger

Sometimes I pray that a meteorite
will hit me. When it doesn't
I just stretch back
beneath the shady branches,
as if to be alone were a privilege

teetering on the edge of sorrow,
although this is the kind of sorrow
we find in the images that sleep
rarely reveals. Sometimes
we know what we are chasing,

sometimes how we are being chased.
And yet we lie beneath the trees and listen,
as if the flowers might sing to us.
And of what would they sing?
The nature of the beautiful?

The illusions of memory? Anything,
I say, that is a little more
than nothing. Even sorrow's slow
irresistible unfolding. Something
is always hurtling toward us from afar.

Objects Have the Longest Memories of All

Don't be fooled by their stillness,
their acquiescence to your touch,
their apparent lack of interest
in that table or shelf or window
looking out on its vacant
prospect. Repetition
has scarred them the way
a few weeks alone in the dark
might loosen you from yourself,
turn you into what you were certain
you could never become. Consider
what they must have witnessed
and now are keeping to themselves:
the hours of interrogation, the false
confessions, the letting go.
And outside: spiky barricades
abandoned in the streets. And this
would only be the smallest part
of the history of their silence—
those coils of wire, that unbroken
watch on a dead man's wrist.
Unfasten it. It will tell you
nothing but the time of day.

Underworld

I won't attempt to describe
the apparitions that led me here,
since deception is in the nature of things—
like the paths I could not trust,

and the labyrinth of circles beneath me,
and the useless clouds above.
Ash was the color of my prayers.
Nor would the angels answer.

I suppose they had their reasons.
Days passed, then years,
as is the case with such journeys.
Therefore I've forgotten

when I stopped looking back,
since I knew I was being followed,
and tested, and found wanting.
As was my father, and his father as well.

As I Walked Out One Morning

I saw a car hit another car.
People gathered, and I couldn't help
but be one of them. "Go home,"
a policeman said. "You've seen enough."

So I did, and soon it was night.
In a park some distance from my house

small ghosts of children drifted
through the circles of the streetlights.
One of them turned toward me.

Then they were gone,
and a man rose from his bench
by the fountain. "These days,"
he said, "they're all around."

"But I don't believe in ghosts," I told him.

"Ah, yes," he replied, "but really
how much difference does that make?"

After he left, the branches of the oaks
and the elms clicked and brushed
against each other. A slice of moon
hovered beyond them. I wondered

what I should or could believe,
or didn't believe
because I hadn't tried.

All around me everything
that was visible—the other
passersby, the edges
of that moon—wavered in my mind.

At home I told my wife
about the accident, and how I came
upon the children in the park.

I didn't say they were ghosts. I said
I couldn't decide
if they were happy or sad.

"Some were," she replied, "some weren't.
They change their minds so often."

She turned the page of a book.
"But why didn't you tell me right away
that they were ghosts?"

I didn't answer.
"Why carry around such a secret," she asked,

"and so deceive yourself into believing
you're alone in all of this, this clutter
and uncertainty, this dubious
pathos, this constant desire to know?"

The Darker Colors

That was the year I was committed to all my bad habits,
like speaking to my friends in riddles and fables
full of apparently irrelevant facts. Did you know
owls are the only animals that can see the color blue?

Did you know iguanas can end their own lives?
What could they be feeling, I asked, to drive them
to such extremes? The blue of twilight
in which the owl traces her swift and soundless circles

is one kind of clue. But did you know
that bats always turn left when exiting a cave?
Hard to believe until you watch for a long time.
So it seemed only right to urge my certainties

on others, who had no time to pay attention,
but recognized, even if they could not respect,
my passion for the unlikely revelations of nature.
Yes, everyone knew I was drawn

to the night and the darker colors: black stripes
of the zebra, fur of the panther, deep water
and fish without eyes. How long, I inquired,
does it take evolution to catch up to our mistakes?

None of us can wait that long.
So you see: when left to my own devices
I made sense, especially alone at the unfolding
of dawn, beside the consistent wash of the sea,

the white heron on one side, the gray on the other,
and around me a flock of sandpipers pretending
to play as children play at the edge of the waves,
as if hunger weren't always their most important thought.

The Variations

At the party someone was saying,
"I don't like insects as much as birds."
Which seemed like the right answer
to a question I hadn't tried to overhear.
Then a woman near me said,
"I didn't realize how much
I cared until it was too late."
In the background Glenn Gould
was playing the *Goldberg Variations*.
He was so young then, in 1955.
Later he plays those pieces more slowly,
but not because he's tired,
though he must have been. It's 1981,
and within a year he'll be dead.
And now it's the day after
Jane told me, "You won't
know anyone at the party, and so
you'll make new friends."
"Yes, a *wood*," the man behind me
insisted. "Different from a forest."
Perhaps I should have asked
exactly how,
but I was distracted by the music
as it suddenly grew quiet
while at the same time refusing
to turn into merely the background
for all of these
different conversations
of all of these friends

I had not yet made. It's likely,
I thought, there are some people
here right now who prefer
other piano players to Glenn Gould.
And for reasons
I would have to respect.
Across the room I could see
that the woman who had failed
to care when she could have
was smiling.
Was she holding back her tears?
But why not
believe I had misunderstood
everything? Jane was making
another guest another drink
when I noticed
the music had ended. Of course
a wood is smaller
than a forest, and regret
is inescapable, even if art
sometimes wishes
it were otherwise,
before showing us
it must be so.

Slowly, Then in a Hurry

Of course you're tired of what we're all tired of:
outrage and confusion, the future
coming to an end, and tired also
of feeling how little it matters to feel this way.
So, yes, go out into the woods,

where everything will appear
more sympathetic—the barely opened
blue and yellow violets, the trilling of birds,
scurryings in the underbrush of small animals
who may be afraid because you're too close.

Then the sun dazzles you into submission,
its radiance reminding you
of that white light those near death have said
beckoned and comforted them until
they woke, but wished to stay. So you leave

the woods feeling no better, worried again
about the hopelessness of worry, and even
the clothes you're wearing, that scarf, for example,
as if its still-vivid colors might single you out
from the others on the street where now

you may be standing, wondering if the man
walking toward you could have you alone
in mind. Yes, this might be death,
if this is what death looks like. Like anybody
coming your way, slowly, then in a hurry.

Spies

But why not think of the world
as a movie you can step into and find yourself
saving someone very beautiful
who might be losing her grip on the edge
of a cliff as you lean
forward to touch her fingers, then grasp
her hand, trying not even for a second
to glance at the landscape
beneath you—the glittering
thread of a river, the edge of the sky.

Meanwhile, the wind tugs at her hair,
toys with her skirt, whispers
of falling, but notice
how neither the man reaching out
nor the woman in danger
seems actually frightened,
because that's the thrill—
being certain you can handle the future.
That's the satisfaction.

I know the story in which you and I
have taken our places
isn't the one we might have chosen—
that movie with precisely
the right amount of peril
and deception and dangerous driving
and then an ending where she says
she'd like to make herself

more comfortable, shrugging off
her jacket, then maybe
unbuttoning her blouse, tossing it
casually across a chair.

Isn't the actual future too easy to imagine?
The daily tasks, the repetitions, and pretty soon
we're asleep long before midnight.
Are you dreaming of yourself in a different life,
of us together in our different lives?

Maybe we've just been shown to the best table
in a grand hotel, snow in the distance
crashing through the mountain passes,
but no one is worried,
the great fire shining in the tall fluted glasses,
the waiter arriving to tell us
everything's been taken care of.

Don't laugh. Why shouldn't we be spies?—
the way I'm whispering to you, the way
you're smoothing your dress
and leaning toward me.
We have our secrets. We could be
two strangers, my dear, thrown together by chance
as once we were—reckless, unafraid,
one step ahead of the past.

Acknowledgments

Grateful acknowledgement is made to the following publications in which these poems first appeared:

Body
"Replicas"

The Common
"An Education" and "In the Natural World"

The Cortland Review
"A Difficult Assignment"

The Idaho Review
"Swimming in the Air"

Lake Effect
"Devotion" and "A Theory of Impossible Objects"

Margie
"Invisible"

The Missouri Review
"The Poem about the Henhouse"

Phantom Drift
"Sunrise with Sea Monsters"

Plume
"Five Parables," "Let Me Tell You What to Feel," "Spies," "Until Evening," and "What Death Said"

River Styx
"Everything That Isn't Happening Here"

The Saranac Review
"It Appeared There Was a Story"

"Being a Monster" appears in the anthology *Outsiders: Poems about Rebels, Exiles, and Renegades,* edited by Laure-Anne Bosselaar (Milkweed Editions, 1999).

Many thanks also to Williams College, Yaddo, and the MacDowell Colony for their continuing support.